MAC.

PERU 2024

TRAVEL GUIDE

Machu Picchu & Beyond: Your made
easy companion and Insider's Guide
for a Smooth planning,budgeting
Tips for an unforgettable journey to
Peru in 2024

By Carolina j. Smith

TABLE OF CONTENTS

INTRODUCTION

Welcome to Machu Picchu, one of the most iconic and awe-inspiring destinations in the world. Whether you're a seasoned traveler or embarking on your first adventure, the allure of Machu Picchu is undeniable. But why visit Machu Picchu? What draws people from all corners of the globe to this remote corner of Peru?

For me, the journey to Machu Picchu began with a simple curiosity—a desire to explore a place steeped in history and mystery. I had seen countless photos and heard tales of its ancient ruins nestled amidst the Andean mountains, but nothing could prepare me for the breathtaking beauty and sense of wonder that awaited me.

It was during my first visit to Machu Picchu that I felt a profound connection to the land and its people. As I stood atop the terraced fields, gazing out at the mist-shrouded peaks, I couldn't help but marvel at the ingenuity of the Inca civilization and the timeless beauty of this sacred site.

But my journey didn't end there. Over the years, I returned to Machu Picchu time and time again, each visit deepening my appreciation for its rich history and cultural significance. And now, I'm thrilled to share my passion for this remarkable destination with you through this guide.

About This Guide

In this book, you'll find everything you need to know to plan your own unforgettable journey to Machu Picchu and the surrounding region. From practical travel tips and insider recommendations to insights into the local cuisine and cultural experiences, this guide is your ticket to exploring the wonders of Machu Picchu like never before.

But more than just a guidebook, this is an invitation to embark on a journey of discovery—a journey that will take you beyond the beaten path and into the heart of one of the world's most captivating destinations. So join me as we explore the ancient ruins, trek through the Andean mountains, and immerse ourselves in the vibrant culture of Peru.

Are you prepared to discover Machu Picchu's magic?
Flip the page and embark on an exciting journey.

Chapter 2 planning your trip

Best time to visit

Planning Your Trip - Best Time to Visit

Planning a trip to Machu Picchu is an exhilarating adventure filled with anticipation and excitement. One of the first decisions you'll need to make is determining the best time to visit this iconic destination. As I embarked on my own journey to Machu Picchu, I grappled with this decision, weighing the pros and cons of each season.

I discovered the following along the way:

High Season (May to September):

The high season in Machu Picchu coincides with the dry season in the Andes, making it the most popular time to visit. During my research, I discovered that this period offers clear skies, minimal rainfall, and warmer temperatures, creating ideal conditions for exploring the ancient ruins. However, I also learned that the high season comes with its drawbacks, namely large crowds and higher prices for accommodations and tours. Despite these challenges, I ultimately decided to visit Machu Picchu during the high season to take advantage of the favorable weather and maximize my chances of clear views.

Shoulder Seasons (April and October):

As I delved deeper into my trip planning, I discovered the shoulder seasons, which offer a middle ground between the high and low seasons. In April and October, the weather is still relatively pleasant, with fewer crowds compared to the peak months. While there may be some rain showers, especially in April, I found that the smaller crowds and lower prices for accommodations made the shoulder seasons an attractive option for visiting Machu Picchu. Ultimately, I decided to keep the shoulder seasons in mind as potential alternatives to the high season, depending on my schedule and preferences.

Low Season (November to March):

Finally, I explored the low season, which occurs during the rainy season in the Andes. While the weather may be less than ideal, with frequent rain showers and cooler temperatures, I discovered that the low season also offers its own unique benefits. With fewer tourists and lower prices for accommodations and tours, I realized that the low season could be an excellent opportunity to experience Machu Picchu without the crowds. However, I knew that I would need to pack appropriate rain gear and be prepared for the possibility of trail closures due to heavy rainfall if I chose to visit during this time.

In the end, I weighed the pros and cons of each season and carefully considered my preferences for crowds and weather. Ultimately, I decided to visit Machu Picchu during the high season to take advantage of the favorable weather and maximize my chances of clear views. However, I kept the shoulder seasons in mind as potential alternatives, depending on my schedule and preferences.

As you plan your own trip to Machu Picchu, I encourage you to consider your priorities and preferences carefully. Whether you choose to visit during the high season, shoulder seasons, or low season, each time of year offers its own unique advantages and challenges. By planning ahead and considering all your options, you'll be well-prepared to embark on an unforgettable journey to this incredible destination.

Entry Requirements and Travel Documents

Before embarking on your journey to Machu Picchu, it's crucial to understand the entry requirements and necessary travel documents for Peru, the country where Machu Picchu is located. This chapter will guide you through the essential information you need to know to ensure a smooth and hassle-free travel experience.

Entry Requirements:
Most visitors to Peru require a passport that is currently valid for at least six months beyond the date of their intended stay.
However, entry requirements may vary depending on your country of citizenship, so it's essential to check the specific requirements for your nationality. Some travelers may also need to obtain a visa before traveling to Peru, while others are eligible for visa-free entry or can

obtain a visa upon arrival. Check with the nearest Peruvian embassy or consulate to confirm the entry requirements for your country.

Travel Documents to Machu Picchu

When planning your visit to Machu Picchu, it's essential to ensure you have the necessary travel documents to enter the site and explore the surrounding area. Here are the key documents you'll need:

Passport: A valid passport is required for all travelers visiting Machu Picchu, regardless of nationality. Make sure your passport is valid for at least six months beyond your intended departure date from Peru.

Visas: travelers from many countries do not need a visa to enter Peru for tourism purposes, including visiting Machu Picchu. However, it's crucial to verify the specific entry requirements based on your nationality, as visa policies can vary and may change over time. Most travelers to Machu Picchu and Peru will need a valid passport with at least six months' validity beyond the intended stay, as well as proof of onward travel and enough money to sustain themselves while t hey are there. Additionally, some travelers may be required to obtain a tourist card upon arrival in Peru. It's always advisable to check with the nearest Peruvian embassy or consulate or consult official government websites for the most up-to-date information on visa requirements before traveling.

Machu Picchu Entrance Ticket: All visitors to Machu Picchu must have a valid entrance ticket to access the archaeological site. You can purchase tickets online in advance through the official government website or at designated ticket offices in Cusco, Aguas Calientes, or Ollantaytambo.

Inca Trail Permit (if applicable): If you plan to hike the classic Inca Trail to Machu Picchu, you'll need to obtain a permit from the Peruvian government. These permits are limited and must be purchased through authorized tour operators well in advance, as they often sell out months in advance.

Train Tickets (if applicable): If you're taking the train to Aguas Calientes, the gateway town to Machu Picchu, you'll need to have your train tickets booked in advance. You can purchase train tickets online through the Peru Rail or Inca Rail websites or through authorized travel agencies in Cusco or other major cities.

Bus Tickets (if applicable): To reach the entrance of Machu Picchu from Aguas Calientes, you'll need to take a bus ride up the winding road to the archaeological site. Bus tickets can be purchased in Aguas Calientes, either in advance or on the day of your visit.

Travel Insurance: While not a mandatory requirement, it's highly recommended to have travel insurance that covers medical emergencies, trip cancellations, and other unforeseen circumstances.
Check your policy to be sure you have enough

Coverage for your trip to Machu Picchu.

Student ID (if applicable): If you're a student under the age of 25, you may be eligible for discounted entrance fees to Machu Picchu and other archaeological sites in Peru. Make sure to bring a valid student ID card to prove your eligibility for the discount.

Before your trip, double-check that you have all the necessary travel documents and keep them safe and easily accessible throughout your journey to Machu Picchu. With proper planning and preparation, you can enjoy a smooth and memorable visit to this iconic archaeological wonder of the world.

In addition to a valid passport and any required visas, there are several other travel documents you may need for your trip to Machu Picchu. If you plan to visit Machu Picchu as part of a guided tour or trek, you may need to obtain special permits or passes in advance. For example, popular trekking routes like the Inca Trail have limited daily quotas, so it's essential to book permits well in advance to secure your spot. Additionally, some documents, such as proof of onward travel and travel insurance, may be required by immigration officials upon arrival in Peru.

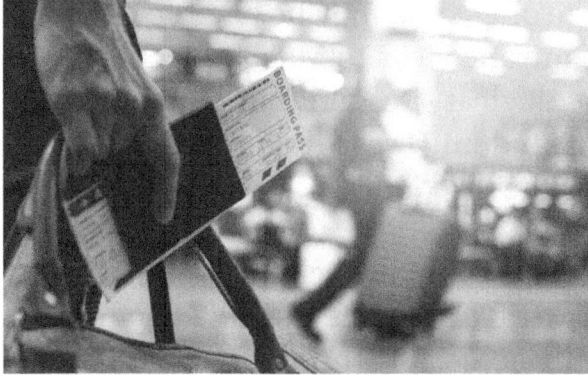

Practical Tips:

Check Entry Requirements Early: Start researching the entry requirements for Peru as soon as you begin planning your trip to Machu Picchu. This will give you plenty of time to obtain any necessary visas or permits and ensure that your passport is up to date.

Keep Important Documents Safe: Make photocopies or digital scans of your passport, visa, and other important travel documents, and keep them in a separate location from the originals. This will come in handy in case your documents are lost or stolen while traveling.

Research Permits and Passes: If you plan to visit Machu Picchu as part of a guided tour or trek, be sure to research any permits or passes that may be required in advance. Book these permits as early as possible to avoid disappointment, especially if you plan to visit during the high season.

By familiarizing yourself with the entry requirements and necessary travel documents for Machu Picchu, you'll be well-prepared to embark on your journey to this incredible destination. Take the time to research and plan ahead, and you'll ensure a smooth and hassle free travel experience from start to finish.

Budgeting and Currency Tips

When planning your trip to Machu Picchu, it's essential to consider your budget and how to manage your expenses while traveling. This chapter will provide you with practical tips on budgeting and handling currency to make the most of your experience without breaking the bank.

Budgeting Tips:

Set a Daily Budget: Before you depart, determine how much you're willing to spend each day on accommodation, meals, transportation, and activities. Be realistic about your expenses and stick to your budget to avoid overspending.

Research Costs: Research the average costs of accommodation, meals, and activities in Machu Picchu to get an idea of how much you'll need to budget.
Remember that costs can change based on the time of year and where you are.

Prioritize Experiences: Allocate your budget towards experiences that matter most to you, such as guided tours, trekking, or cultural activities. Focus on creating memorable experiences rather than unnecessary expenses.

Currency Tips:

Know the Local Currency: The official currency of Peru is the Peruvian Sol (PEN). Familiarize yourself with the current exchange rate to avoid confusion when making purchases.

Carry Cash: While credit cards are widely accepted in tourist areas, cash is still king in many places, especially in rural areas or markets. Be sure to carry small denominations of Sol for convenience.

Exchange Currency Wisely: Exchange currency at banks or authorized exchange offices to get the best rates.
Don't exchange money at hotels or airports; they usually give higher exchange rates.

Practical Tips:

Use ATMs Wisely: ATMs are readily available in major cities and towns in Peru. Withdraw larger amounts of cash to minimize transaction fees, but be cautious of using ATMs in remote areas, as they may be limited.

Monitor Exchange Rates: Keep an eye on exchange rates leading up to your trip and consider exchanging currency when rates are favorable. However, avoid exchanging too much money at once to minimize the risk of carrying large sums of cash.

Budget for Tips: While tipping is not mandatory in Peru, it's customary to tip for exceptional service in restaurants and for tour guides. Factor in tipping expenses when budgeting for your trip.

By following these budgeting and currency tips, you'll be better prepared to manage your expenses and make the most of your trip to Machu Picchu. Remember to plan ahead, stick to your budget, and prioritize experiences that will make your journey truly memorable.

Packing Essentials for Your Machu Picchu Adventure

Preparing for your Machu Picchu adventure requires careful consideration of what to pack to ensure you're comfortable and prepared for the various conditions you may encounter. This chapter will outline the essential items you'll need to pack for your trip to Machu Picchu, along with practical tips to help you make the most of your experience.

Clothing:

Layered Clothing: Machu Picchu's weather can be unpredictable, with temperatures fluctuating throughout the day. Pack lightweight, moisture-wicking clothing that can be easily layered to adapt to changing conditions.

Waterproof Jacket: Rain showers are common, especially during the rainy season. A waterproof jacket will help keep you dry and comfortable while exploring the ruins and trekking through the Andean mountains.

Sturdy Hiking Boots: Comfortable and supportive hiking boots are essential for exploring Machu Picchu's rugged terrain. Choose boots with good traction to navigate slippery trails and uneven terrain.

Sun Protection: The sun's rays can be strong at high altitudes. Pack sunglasses, a widebrimmed hat, and sunscreen with high SPF to protect yourself from sunburn and UV damage.

Gear and Accessories:

Daypack: A lightweight daypack is essential for carrying water, snacks, and other essentials during your excursions. Look for a pack with comfortable straps and multiple compartments for easy organization.

Water Bottle:
Carry a reusable water bottle to stay hydrated. Consider a bottle with a built-in filter to purify water from streams or refilling stations along the trails.

Camera or Smartphone: Capture the breathtaking scenery and memorable moments of your Machu Picchu adventure with a camera or smartphone.
To keep your devices charged, don't forget to
 Pack extra batteries or a portable charger.

Snacks: Pack energy-boosting snacks like trail mix, granola bars, and dried fruit to keep you fueled during long hikes and exploration.

Practical Tips:

Pack Light: While it's essential to be prepared, avoid over packing. Stick to the essentials and prioritize lightweight, versatile clothing and gear to minimize the weight of your backpack.

Check the Weather Forecast: Keep an eye on the weather forecast leading up to your trip and pack accordingly. Be prepared for both rain and sunshine, and dress in layers to stay comfortable throughout the day.

Dress Appropriately: Machu Picchu's terrain can be challenging, so wear comfortable clothing and sturdy footwear suitable for hiking and walking long distances.

By packing these essential items and following these practical tips, you'll be well-prepared to embark on your Machu Picchu adventure. Remember to plan ahead, pack wisely, and most importantly, enjoy every moment of your journey to this incredible destination.

Crafting Your Itinerary

Crafting a well-planned itinerary is key to making the most of your Machu Picchu adventure. In this chapter, we'll explore how to create a balanced and enjoyable itinerary that allows you to experience the highlights of Machu Picchu while also leaving room for flexibility and spontaneity.

Research and Prioritize Attractions: Start by researching the various attractions and activities available at Machu Picchu, such as the main ruins, hiking trails, and cultural experiences. Consider your interests, preferences, and time constraints when prioritizing which attractions to include in your itinerary.

Allocate Time Wisely: Be realistic about how much time you'll need to explore each attraction and factor in travel time between sites. Remember to account for breaks, meals, and rest periods to avoid feeling rushed or overwhelmed.

Consider Seasonal Factors: Take into account seasonal factors such as weather conditions, crowd levels, and daylight hours when planning your itinerary. For example, if you're visiting during the high season, you may need to book popular attractions and accommodations in advance to secure your spot.

Plan for Flexibility: While it's important to have a structured itinerary, leave room for flexibility to accommodate unexpected changes or opportunities that may arise during your trip. Allow yourself the freedom to explore off-the beaten-path attractions or to spend more time at places that capture your interest.

Include Downtime: Don't forget to schedule downtime in your itinerary to rest and recharge. Machu Picchu can be physically demanding, especially if you plan to hike or trek, so be sure to listen to your body and take breaks as needed.

Practical Tips:

Use a Calendar or Spreadsheet: Create a detailed itinerary using a calendar or spreadsheet, outlining each day's activities, transportation, and accommodations. You'll be more organised and won't lose any crucial information if you do this.

Check Opening Hours and Availability:
Before finalizing your itinerary, double-check
the opening hours and availability of attractions
and tours. Some sites may have limited hours or
require advanced reservations, so it's essential to
plan accordingly.

Seek Local Advice: Consider seeking advice
from locals or experienced travelers who have
visited Machu Picchu before. They may offer
valuable insights and recommendations for off
the-beaten-path attractions or hidden gems to
include in your itinerary.

Be Realistic: While it's tempting to try to fit in
as much as possible, be realistic about what you
can realistically accomplish in a day. Avoid
overloading your itinerary with too many
activities or attractions, as this can lead to
burnout and disappointment.

By following these practical tips and guidelines,
you'll be able to craft a well-rounded and
enjoyable itinerary that allows you to make the
most of your Machu Picchu adventure.
Remember to plan ahead, stay flexible, and most
importantly, savor every moment of your
journey to this incredible destination

Chapter 3

Getting to Machu Picchu

Transportation Options

Getting to Machu Picchu, the iconic Incan citadel nestled in the Peruvian Andes, is an adventure in itself. Whether you're arriving from Cusco, Ollantaytambo, or other nearby towns, several transportation options are available to suit your preferences and budget.

1. Train:

One of the most popular and convenient ways to reach Machu Picchu is by train. The Peru Rail and Inca Rail companies offer scenic train journeys from Cusco, Ollantaytambo, and the Sacred Valley to Aguas Calientes, the gateway town to Machu Picchu. The train ride provides stunning views of the Andean landscape and lush valleys, making it a memorable part of your Machu Picchu experience.

Practical Tip: Book your train tickets in advance, especially during peak tourist seasons, to secure your preferred departure time and seating class.

2. Hiking Trails:

For adventurous travelers seeking a more immersive experience, several hiking trails lead to Machu Picchu, including the famous Inca

Trail, Salkantay Trek, and Lares Trek. These multi-day hikes offer breathtaking scenery, ancient Incan ruins, and opportunities to connect with nature along the way. While the trails vary in difficulty and duration, each offers a unique perspective on the Andean landscape and cultural heritage of the region.

Practical Tip: If you plan to hike to Machu Picchu, make sure to obtain the necessary permits and plan your trek well in advance. Pack appropriate gear, including sturdy hiking boots, rain gear, and a reliable daypack.

3. Bus:

From Aguas Calientes, travelers can take a short bus ride up the winding road to the entrance of Machu Picchu. The bus journey offers panoramic views of the surrounding mountains and valleys, providing a convenient and comfortable way to reach the archaeological site without the need for strenuous hiking.

Practical Tip: Purchase your bus tickets in advance or upon arrival in Aguas Calientes to avoid long waits at the bus station, especially during peak hours.

4. Combination Tours:

Many tour operators offer combination packages that include transportation, entrance tickets, guided tours, and other amenities for a hassle-free Machu Picchu experience. These tours often provide transportation from Cusco or other nearby towns, allowing travelers to relax and enjoy the journey while expert guides take care of the logistics.

Practical Tip: Research and compare different tour packages to find one that suits your interests, budget, and travel preferences. Look for reputable operators with positive reviews and a commitment to sustainable tourism practices.

No matter which transportation option you choose, reaching Machu Picchu is sure to be a highlight of your trip to Peru. From scenic train rides to adventurous treks, each journey offers a unique perspective on the awe-inspiring beauty and cultural significance of this ancient wonder of the world. So sit back, relax, and get ready to embark on an unforgettable adventure to Machu Picchu!

5.Private Transportation: Private taxis or vans can also be hired for a direct transfer from Cusco to the entrance of Machu Picchu. This option is convenient for travelers who prefer a more flexible schedule or want to explore the surrounding area at their own pace.

While there is no direct flight to Machu Picchu, travelers can fly into Alejandro Velasco Astete International Airport in Cusco from major cities in Peru, as well as from some international destinations such as Lima, La Paz, and Bogota. From Cusco, various transportation options are available to complete the journey to Machu Picchu.

Accommodation Choices

When planning your visit to Machu Picchu, choosing the right accommodation is essential for a comfortable and enjoyable experience. From luxury hotels to budget-friendly hostels, there are various options to suit every traveler's preferences and budget.

1. Hotels:

There are several hotels located in Aguas Calientes, the gateway town to Machu Picchu. These hotels offer a range of amenities, including comfortable rooms, onsite restaurants, and sometimes even spa facilities. Some hotels also provide stunning views of the surrounding mountains and rivers, adding to the overall experience.

Practical Tip: Book your hotel accommodation well in advance, especially during peak tourist seasons, to secure your preferred dates and room type. Consider staying in a hotel that offers shuttle services to and from Machu Picchu to save time and hassle.

2. Hostels and Guesthouses:

For budget-conscious travelers, hostels and guesthouses in Aguas Calientes provide affordable accommodation options. These establishments typically offer dormitory-style rooms with shared bathrooms, as well as private rooms with ensuite facilities. While amenities may be more basic compared to hotels, hostels and guesthouses are a great choice for those looking to save money while still enjoying a comfortable stay.

Practical Tip: Check online reviews and ratings before booking a hostel or guesthouse to ensure cleanliness, safety, and good value for money. Look for accommodations with positive feedback from previous guests and convenient locations within walking distance of the town center.

3. Eco-Lodges:

For travelers seeking a more sustainable and eco-friendly accommodation option, there are several eco-lodges located in the Sacred Valley region near Machu Picchu. These lodges prioritize environmental conservation and offer immersive experiences that connect guests with nature and local communities. From rustic cabins to luxury tents, eco-lodges provide a unique and off-the-grid experience for adventurous travelers.

Practical Tip: Research eco-lodges in advance to find one that aligns with your values and interests. Consider participating in eco-friendly activities offered by the lodge, such as guided nature walks, organic farming, or cultural exchanges with local communities.

4. Camping:

For the ultimate outdoor adventure, camping near Machu Picchu is an option for those looking to immerse themselves in nature. There are designated campsites along the Inca Trail and other hiking routes leading to Machu Picchu, as well as campsites in the surrounding Sacred Valley area. While camping requires more preparation and equipment, it allows travelers to experience the beauty of the Andean landscape up close.

Practical Tip: If you plan to camp, make sure to obtain the necessary permits and equipment in advance. Pack lightweight camping gear, including a sturdy tent, sleeping bag, cooking supplies, and appropriate clothing for varying weather conditions.

No matter which accommodation option you choose, make sure to book in advance and consider factors such as location, amenities, and budget to ensure a comfortable and enjoyable stay during your visit to Machu Picchu.

Guided Tours vs. Independent Travel

When planning your visit to Machu Picchu, one of the decisions you'll need to make is whether to join a guided tour or explore independently. Both options offer unique advantages and considerations, so let's explore the differences to help you make an informed choice.

1. Guided Tours:

Guided tours provide a structured and educational experience led by knowledgeable local guides.
The following are some advantages of taking a guided tour

Expert Insight: Local guides offer in-depth knowledge about Machu Picchu's history, culture, and significance. They can provide valuable insights and answer questions, enriching your understanding of the archaeological site.

Convenience: Guided tours typically include transportation, entrance tickets, and sometimes meals, making them a convenient option for travelers who prefer a hassle-free experience. You can relax and enjoy the journey while the tour operator takes care of the logistics.

Safety: Traveling with a guided tour reduces the risk of getting lost or encountering difficulties, especially for first-time visitors. Guides are familiar with the terrain and can navigate efficiently, ensuring a smooth and secure visit.

Practical Tip: Research different guided tour operators and read reviews from previous participants to find a reputable and reliable company. Consider factors such as group size, itinerary, and quality of guides when making your decision.

2. Independent Travel:

Independent travel allows you to explore Machu Picchu at your own pace and on your terms. Here are some reasons why you might choose independent travel:

Flexibility: Independent travelers have the freedom to create their own itinerary, spend as much time as they like at each site, and explore off-the-beaten-path areas.
Your experience can be created for your preferences and areas of interest.

Cost Savings: Traveling independently can be more budget-friendly compared to joining a guided tour, especially if you're willing to research and book transportation, accommodation, and entrance tickets yourself. You have more control over your expenses and can choose budget-friendly options.

Personal Discovery: Exploring Machu Picchu independently allows for a deeper sense of discovery and connection with the site. You can wander at your own pace, soak in the atmosphere, and uncover hidden gems without the constraints of a group itinerary.

Practical Tip: Plan your itinerary in advance and familiarize yourself with Machu Picchu's layout, hiking trails, and points of interest. Bring a guidebook or download a digital guide to enhance your understanding of the site's history and significance.

Considerations for Both Options:

Crowds: Machu Picchu is a popular tourist destination, and both guided tours and independent travelers may encounter crowds, especially during peak seasons. Consider visiting during off-peak times or early in the morning to avoid the busiest times of day.

Responsible Travel: Whether you choose a guided tour or independent travel, remember to practice responsible tourism by respecting the environment, following local regulations, and supporting sustainable tourism practices.

The choice between a self-sufficient trip and a guided tour ultimately comes down to personal taste, financial situation, and mode of transportation.
Whichever option you choose, Machu Picchu promises an unforgettable experience filled with awe-inspiring landscapes, ancient ruins, and cultural richness.

Chapter 4

Exploring Machu Picchu

Attractions Center

Machu Picchu, with its breathtaking beauty and rich history, offers a plethora of attractions to explore. From ancient ruins to panoramic viewpoints, here are some of the key attractions you won't want to miss during your visit:

1. The Citadel:

At the heart of Machu Picchu lies the ancient citadel, a UNESCO World Heritage site and one of the New Seven Wonders of the World. Explore the meticulously crafted stone structures, including temples, terraces, and residential areas, and marvel at the ingenuity of the Inca civilization. Highlights include the Temple of the Sun, the Intihuatana stone, and the iconic agricultural terraces.

Practical Tip: Start your visit early in the morning to avoid the crowds and experience the citadel in the soft morning light. Consider hiring a local guide to provide insights into the history and significance of each structure.

2. Huayna Picchu and Machu Picchu Mountain:

For panoramic views of Machu Picchu and the surrounding Andean landscape, consider hiking to the summit of Huayna Picchu or Machu Picchu Mountain. These challenging hikes offer unparalleled vantage points and the opportunity to appreciate the scale and grandeur of the citadel from above.

Practical Tip: Huayna Picchu permits are limited and sell out quickly, so make sure to book your permit well in advance if you plan to hike. Machu Picchu Mountain permits are also limited but may be easier to secure.

3. Temple of the Condor:

Discover the enigmatic Temple of the Condor, an ancient structure shaped like a giant condor with outstretched wings. This unique site is believed to have served as a ceremonial space for rituals and offerings, with its intricate stone carvings representing the sacred bird of the Andes.

Practical Tip: Take your time to explore the details of the Temple of the Condor and imagine the rituals that once took place within its walls. Be respectful of the site and avoid touching or climbing on the delicate stone carvings.

4. Sun Gate (Inti Punku):

For those who have completed the Inca Trail trek, the Sun Gate offers a memorable entrance to Machu Picchu. This stone gateway marks the final stretch of the trail and provides stunning views of the citadel and surrounding mountains. It's the perfect spot to pause and reflect on your journey before descending into Machu Picchu.

Practical Tip: Arrive at the Sun Gate early in the morning or late in the afternoon for the best lighting and fewer crowds. Take plenty of photos to commemorate your achievement and soak in the beauty of the landscape.

Exploring Machu Picchu is a once-in-a-lifetime experience that promises awe-inspiring sights and unforgettable moments. Whether you're admiring the ancient ruins of the citadel, hiking to panoramic viewpoints, or marveling at the intricate stone carvings, Machu Picchu offers something magical for every visitor to discover.

History and Significance

Machu Picchu's history and significance are as captivating as its stunning landscapes. Understanding the story behind this ancient citadel adds depth to your visit and allows you to appreciate its cultural importance. Let's delve into the history and significance of Machu Picchu:

1. History:

During the reign of Emperor Pachacuti in the fifteenth century, the Inca civilization established Machu Picchu. It served as a royal estate and religious sanctuary, nestled high in the Andes mountains of Peru. The site was inhabited for approximately 100 years before being abandoned, likely due to the Spanish conquest and subsequent colonization.

Practical Tip: Engage with local guides or audio guides available at the site to learn more about Machu Picchu's history as you explore the ruins. Look for signage and interpretive displays that provide insights into the site's construction, purpose, and eventual rediscovery.

2. Rediscovery:

For generations, Machu Picchu was concealed fr om the outer world. It weren't until 1911 that American explorer Hiram Bingham discovered it again. Bingham stumbled upon the site while searching for the lost city of Vilcabamba and was struck by its grandeur and mystery. His expeditions and subsequent publications brought international attention to Machu Picchu and sparked interest in Inca archaeology.

Practical Tip: Visit the onsite museum in Machu Picchu to learn more about Hiram Bingham's expeditions and the process of rediscovering the citadel. Explore exhibits showcasing artifacts, photographs, and historical documents related to Machu Picchu's excavation and preservation.

3. Cultural Significance:

Machu Picchu holds immense cultural significance as a symbol of Inca ingenuity, spirituality, and resilience. Its precise architectural design, sophisticated agricultural terraces, and astronomical alignments reflect the Inca's deep connection to the natural world and their reverence for the cosmos. The site's location amidst towering mountains and lush valleys further enhances its spiritual aura and sense of awe.

Practical Tip: Take a moment to absorb the energy and atmosphere of Machu Picchu as you explore its ancient ruins and scenic vistas. Consider participating in a guided meditation or yoga session offered at the site to connect with its spiritual essence and find inner peace amidst the surrounding beauty.

4. UNESCO World Heritage Site:

Machu Picchu was named a UNESCO World heritage Site in 1983 in honor of its cultural and historical significance. This prestigious designation ensures the preservation and protection of the site for future generations to enjoy and learn from. Machu Picchu continues to inspire awe and wonder in visitors from around the world, serving as a testament to the enduring legacy of the Inca civilization.

Practical Tip: Support responsible tourism practices by respecting Machu Picchu's rules and regulations, such as staying on designated trails, refraining from touching or climbing on the ruins, and disposing of waste properly. By being mindful of your impact, you contribute to the preservation of Machu Picchu for future generations to experience and appreciate.

Understanding the history and significance of Machu Picchu adds depth to your visit and allows you to connect with its cultural heritage on a deeper level. As you explore the ancient ruins and breathtaking landscapes, take a moment to reflect on the legacy of the Inca civilization and the enduring beauty of this iconic wonder of the world.

Archaeological Sites and Landmarks

Machu Picchu is not only a singular archaeological site but also surrounded by several other intriguing landmarks and ruins that add depth to your exploration. Let's delve into some of these remarkable archaeological sites and landmarks:

1. Temple of the Sun:

One of the most impressive structures within Machu Picchu is the Temple of the Sun, dedicated to the Inca sun god Inti. Located in the urban sector of the citadel, this sacred temple features meticulously crafted stonework and a semi-circular tower believed to have been an astronomical observatory.

Practical Tip: Visit the Temple of the Sun during the early morning or late afternoon when the sunlight illuminates the temple's interior, highlighting its architectural precision and spiritual significance.

2. Intihuatana Stone:

Near the Temple of the Sun stands the enigmatic Intihuatana Stone, an intricately carved granite rock that served as a ceremonial object for astronomical observation and ritual ceremonies. Believed to have been used by the Inca to measure the passing of time and the changing seasons, the Intihuatana Stone holds profound cultural and spiritual significance.

Practical Tip: Take a moment to observe the intricate carvings on the Intihuatana Stone and contemplate its role in the spiritual beliefs and practices of the Inca civilization.

3. Temple of the Condor:

Another fascinating structure within Machu Picchu is the Temple of the Condor, named for its resemblance to the wingspan of a condor in flight. This natural rock formation was skillfully shaped by the Inca into the likeness of the revered Andean bird, symbolizing power, freedom, and spirituality.

Practical Tip: Explore the Temple of the Condor and marvel at the ingenuity of the Inca craftsmen who transformed the natural rock formations into sacred architectural masterpieces.

4. The Sacred Plaza:

At the heart of Machu Picchu lies the Sacred Plaza, a central square surrounded by important ceremonial and administrative buildings. This sacred space served as the spiritual and political hub of the citadel, where rituals, ceremonies, and gatherings took place amidst the awe inspiring backdrop of the surrounding mountains.

Practical Tip: Take your time to wander through the Sacred Plaza and imagine the bustling activity that once filled this sacred space during the height of the Inca civilization.

5. Inca Bridge:

Located on the eastern side of Machu Picchu, the Inca Bridge is a remarkable engineering feat that demonstrates the Inca's mastery of stone construction and strategic planning. This narrow pathway carved into the Cliff side served as a secret entrance and defensive barrier, providing access to Machu Picchu while deterring intruders.

Practical Tip: For adventurous travelers, hike to the Inca Bridge and marvel at the breathtaking views of the surrounding valleys and mountains along the way. Exercise caution while traversing the narrow pathway, as it may be challenging for those with a fear of heights.

Exploring these archaeological sites and landmarks within Machu Picchu offers a glimpse into the rich cultural heritage and architectural brilliance of the Inca civilization. As you wander through the ancient ruins and soak in the awe inspiring scenery, take time to appreciate the profound legacy of this iconic wonder of the world.

Hiking and Trekking Routes

Machu Picchu offers a plethora of hiking and trekking routes that cater to adventurers of all levels. Whether you're seeking a challenging multi-day trek or a leisurely day hike, there's a route to suit your preferences. Let's explore some of the most popular hiking and trekking options:

1. Inca Trail:

The classic Inca Trail is perhaps the most famous trekking route to Machu Picchu, offering a challenging yet rewarding journey through breathtaking Andean landscapes and ancient Inca ruins. The trail typically takes four days to complete and covers approximately 43 kilometers (26 miles) of terrain, culminating in a spectacular sunrise view of Machu Picchu from the Sun Gate.

Practical Tip: Book your Inca Trail permits well in advance, as they are limited and tend to sell out months in advance, especially during the peak trekking season from May to September. Ensure you are adequately prepared for the physical demands of the trek, including acclimatizing to the altitude and packing appropriate gear.

2. Salkantay Trek:

For those seeking an alternative to the Inca Trail, the Salkantay Trek offers a challenging and scenic route through diverse ecosystems, including snow-capped mountains, lush cloud forests, and subtropical valleys. The trek typically takes five days to complete and culminates with a breathtaking view of Machu Picchu from the Salkantay Pass.

Practical Tip: Consider joining a guided tour for the Salkantay Trek, as the route can be challenging to navigate independently. Be prepared for fluctuating weather conditions, including cold temperatures at higher altitudes and rain in the cloud forest.

3. Lares Trek:

The Lares Trek is a less crowded alternative to the Inca Trail, offering a cultural immersion experience as you hike through remote Andean villages and interact with indigenous Quechua communities. The trek typically takes three to four days to complete and includes visits to traditional markets, hot springs, and ancient archaeological sites along the way.

Practical Tip: Take the time to learn about the customs and traditions of the Quechua communities you encounter along the Lares Trek, and consider supporting local artisans by purchasing handmade crafts and textiles.

4. Day Hikes:

For those short on time or looking for a more leisurely experience, there are several day hike options available in the Machu Picchu area. Popular day hikes include the hike to the Sun Gate for panoramic views of Machu Picchu, the trek to the Inca Bridge for a glimpse of the ancient defensive structure, and the hike to the Mandor Waterfall for a refreshing dip in the natural pools.

Practical Tip: Start your day hike early in the morning to avoid the midday heat and crowds, and bring plenty of water, sunscreen, and snacks to stay hydrated and energized throughout the trek.

No matter which hiking or trekking route you choose, exploring Machu Picchu on foot offers a unique and immersive experience that allows you to connect with the natural beauty and cultural heritage of this iconic destination. Take your time to savor the journey and appreciate the awe-inspiring landscapes that await you along the way.

Wildlife and Natural Wonders

Machu Picchu is not only renowned for its ancient ruins and archaeological sites but also for its rich biodiversity and stunning natural landscapes. As you explore the area surrounding Machu Picchu, keep an eye out for the diverse wildlife and natural wonders that call this region home. Here are some highlights to look out for:

1. Andean Spectacled Bear:

One of the most iconic inhabitants of the Andean region is the Andean spectacled bear, also known as the Paddington bear due to its resemblance to the beloved literary character. These elusive bears are primarily found in the cloud forests and mountainous regions surrounding Machu Picchu, where they feed on a diet of fruits, berries, and vegetation.

Practical Tip: While sightings of Andean spectacled bears are rare, keep your eyes peeled and binoculars ready during your hikes and treks around Machu Picchu. Early morning and late afternoon are the best times to spot wildlife when they are most active.

2. Andean Cock-of-the-rock:

Another highlight of the region's wildlife is the Andean cock-of-the-rock, a vibrant orange bird known for its distinctive mating rituals and flamboyant plumage. Found in the cloud forests and montane forests of the Andes, these birds are often spotted near rocky outcrops and forest clearings.

Practical Tip: Join a guided birdwatching tour or hike to remote areas with experienced guides who can help you spot elusive bird species like the Andean cock-of-the-rock. Bring a pair of binoculars and a field guide to identify birds and other wildlife species.

3. Orchids and Bromeliads:

The cloud forests surrounding Machu Picchu are home to a stunning array of orchids and bromeliads, adding vibrant splashes of color to the lush green landscape. With over 370 orchid species and countless bromeliad varieties, these delicate flowers are a testament to the region's biodiversity and ecological richness.

Practical Tip: Take a leisurely stroll through the cloud forests and keep an eye out for colorful orchids and bromeliads clinging to tree branches and rocks. Consider joining a guided botanical tour to learn more about the diverse flora of the Andean region.

4. Sacred Valley:

Beyond Machu Picchu, the Sacred Valley offers a wealth of natural wonders to explore, including snow-capped peaks, meandering rivers, and fertile agricultural terraces. Visit the picturesque villages of Pisac, Ollantaytambo, and Chinchero to experience the traditional way of life and soak in the stunning scenery.

Practical Tip: Plan a day trip or overnight stay in the Sacred Valley to fully appreciate its natural beauty and cultural heritage. Visit local markets, hike to scenic viewpoints, and immerse yourself in the Andean way of life.

Exploring the wildlife and natural wonders surrounding Machu Picchu adds another dimension to your visit, allowing you to connect with the region's ecological diversity and appreciate the delicate balance of its ecosystems. Keep your senses attuned to the sights and sounds of the Andean landscape, and you'll be rewarded with unforgettable encounters with wildlife and breathtaking vistas.

Chapter 5

Machu Picchu Cuisine

Traditional Peruvian Dishes

Peruvian cuisine is as diverse and vibrant as the country's landscapes, drawing inspiration from indigenous ingredients, Spanish influences, and flavors from around the world. As you explore Machu Picchu and the surrounding region, be sure to sample some of these traditional Peruvian dishes that offer a taste of the local culture:

1. Ceviche: Ceviche is perhaps Peru's most famous dish, featuring fresh raw fish marinated in citrus juices, typically lime or lemon, and seasoned with onions, chili peppers, and cilantro. The acidity of the citrus "cooks" the fish, resulting in a refreshing and zesty seafood dish that is perfect for hot weather.

Practical Tip: Look for cevicherías or seafood restaurants in the towns surrounding Machu Picchu, where you can enjoy freshly prepared ceviche using locally sourced ingredients. Pair it with a cold beer or a classic Peruvian cocktail like the Pisco Sour for a refreshing culinary experience.

2.   Lomo Saltado: Lomo Saltado is a hearty stir-fry dish that combines marinated strips of beef or alpaca with onions, tomatoes, and peppers, seasoned with soy sauce and vinegar. Served with rice and French fries, this fusion dish reflects Peru's diverse culinary heritage and is a favorite comfort food among locals and visitors alike.

Practical Tip: Look for restaurants and street food vendors serving Lomo Saltado in the towns and villages near Machu Picchu, where you can savor this satisfying dish while enjoying views of the surrounding mountains and valleys.

3.   Aji de Gallina: Aji de Gallina is a creamy chicken stew flavored with aji amarillo chili peppers, onions, garlic, and spices, thickened with bread and ground walnuts. This comforting dish has its roots in Spanish colonial cuisine and is often served with boiled potatoes, rice, and hard-boiled eggs.

Practical Tip: Seek out traditional Peruvian restaurants or local eateries in the towns surrounding Machu Picchu to sample Aji de Gallina prepared according to authentic family recipes passed down through generations.

4.   Anticuchos: Anticuchos are skewers of marinated and grilled beef heart, a popular street food dish enjoyed throughout Peru. The beef heart is typically marinated in a spicy sauce made from aji panca chili peppers, vinegar, and garlic before being grilled to perfection over an open flame.

Practical Tip: Look for street food stalls and markets in the towns and villages near Machu Picchu where you can find Anticuchos being grilled to order. Enjoy them as a flavorful and satisfying snack while exploring the local culinary scene.

5.   Pisco Sour: No culinary journey through Peru would be complete without sampling the country's national cocktail, the Pisco Sour. This refreshing and tangy cocktail is made from Pisco, a grape brandy, lime juice, simple syrup, and egg white, shaken together and served ice cold with a dash of bitters on top.

Practical Tip: Enjoy a Pisco Sour as a predinner aperitif or a post-hike refreshment at one of the many bars and restaurants in the towns surrounding Machu Picchu. Sip slowly and savor the unique flavors of Peru's most iconic cocktail.

Exploring the traditional Peruvian dishes of Machu Picchu and the surrounding region offers a delicious glimpse into the country's rich culinary heritage. From fresh seafood ceviche to hearty beef stir-fries and creamy chicken stews, there's something to delight every palate and satisfy every craving. Be sure to indulge in these culinary delights as you immerse yourself in the flavors of Peru.

Local Food Markets and Street Vendors in Machu Picchu, Peru

When exploring Machu Picchu, Peru, one of the best ways to experience the local culture and cuisine is through its vibrant food markets and street vendors. These bustling hubs offer a wide array of delicious dishes and fresh produce, giving visitors a taste of authentic Peruvian flavors.

Exploring the Markets: Machu Picchu boasts several markets where you can immerse yourself in the sights, sounds, and aromas of Peruvian cuisine. The most popular market in town is the Mercado de Abastos, located near the train station. Here, you'll find an abundance of fruits, vegetables, meats, and spices, as well as local handicrafts and souvenirs.

Practical Tips for Navigating the Markets:

Arrive Early: To experience the markets at their liveliest and to get the freshest produce, consider visiting early in the morning when vendors are setting up shop.

Bring Cash: While some vendors may accept credit cards, it's always a good idea to carry cash for easier transactions.

Practice Your Spanish: While many vendors may speak some English, knowing a few basic Spanish phrases can go a long way in communicating and negotiating prices.

Be Adventurous: Don't hesitate to try new foods and flavors. The markets are a great place to sample traditional Peruvian dishes like ceviche, anticuchos (grilled skewers), and empanadas.

Street Food Delights: In addition to the markets, Machu Picchu's streets are lined with

vendors selling an assortment of delectable street food.
There is something to suit every appetite, from sweets to savoury nibbles

Practical Tips for Enjoying Street Food:

Choose Popular Stalls: Look for vendors with a crowd of locals, as this usually indicates that their food is fresh and delicious.

Check for Cleanliness: Before purchasing food from a vendor, take a moment to observe their hygiene practices and the cleanliness of their cooking area.

Ask About Ingredients: If you have any dietary restrictions or allergies, don't hesitate to ask the vendor about the ingredients in their dishes.

Eat Like a Local: Many Peruvians enjoy their street food with a side of ají sauce, made from spicy peppers. Give it a try for an extra kick of flavor.

Conclusion: Exploring the local food markets and street vendors in Machu Picchu is not only a culinary adventure but also a cultural experience. By immersing yourself in the vibrant atmosphere and sampling traditional Peruvian dishes, you'll gain a deeper appreciation for the rich gastronomic heritage of this remarkable region. So don't miss out on the opportunity to tantalize your taste buds and indulge in the flavors of Machu Picchu!

Dining Recommendations and Culinary Experiences

When visiting Machu Picchu, Peru, indulging in the local cuisine is a must. From traditional Peruvian dishes to international fare, there are plenty of dining options to suit every taste and budget. Here are some dining recommendations and culinary experiences to enhance your gastronomic journey in Machu Picchu.

Exploring Local Eateries: Machu Picchu offers a variety of restaurants, cafes, and eateries where you can sample authentic Peruvian flavors.

Practical Tips for Dining Out:

Reserve in Advance: Popular restaurants in Machu Picchu can fill up quickly, especially during peak tourist seasons. It's advisable to make reservations in advance, especially for dinner.

Try Traditional Dishes: Don't miss the opportunity to savor traditional Peruvian dishes such as lomo saltado (stir-fried beef), causa (potato-based dish), and aji de gallina (spicy chicken stew).

Ask for Recommendations: If you're unsure what to order, don't hesitate to ask your server for recommendations. They can often suggest local specialties or house specialties worth trying.

Consider Dietary Restrictions: Many restaurants in Machu Picchu offer vegetarian, vegan, and gluten-free options. If you have dietary restrictions, inform your server, and they can assist you in finding suitable dishes.

Culinary Experiences: In addition to dining at restaurants, Machu Picchu offers various culinary experiences that allow you to learn about and participate in traditional cooking methods and food preparation techniques.

Practical Tips for Culinary Experiences:

Take a Cooking Class: Joining a cooking class is a fun and interactive way to learn how to prepare authentic Peruvian dishes. Classes often include a visit to a local market to purchase ingredients before heading to the kitchen to cook.

Visit a Pachamanca: Pachamanca is a traditional Peruvian cooking method that involves cooking meat, potatoes, and vegetables in an underground oven. Many tour companies offer excursions to rural areas where you can participate in or observe a Pachamanca.

Attend Food Festivals: Keep an eye out for food festivals and culinary events happening in Machu Picchu during your visit. These events often feature local chefs, traditional music and dance performances, and, of course, plenty of delicious food to sample.

Conclusion: Exploring dining recommendations and culinary experiences in Machu Picchu is an integral part of experiencing the local culture and cuisine. Whether you're dining at a traditional Peruvian restaurant or participating in a cooking class, there are plenty of opportunities to indulge in delicious food and immerse yourself in the vibrant gastronomic scene of this iconic destination. So be sure to savor every bite and enjoy the culinary delights that Machu Picchu has to offer!

Chapter 6

Cultural Experiences - Traditional Customs and Festivals

Immersing yourself in the cultural heritage of Machu Picchu, Peru, goes beyond exploring its ancient ruins. Traditional customs and festivals offer a deeper understanding of the local way of life and provide memorable experiences for visitors.

Exploring Traditional Customs: Machu Picchu is home to various indigenous communities, each with its own customs and traditions passed down through generations. Engaging with these customs allows visitors to gain insight into the rich cultural tapestry of the region.

Practical Tips for Engaging with Traditional Customs:

Respect Local Traditions: When participating in traditional customs or rituals, it's essential to show respect for the cultural significance they hold. Observe and follow the guidance of local community members to ensure you're participating respectfully.

Ask Questions: Don't hesitate to ask questions about the customs you're witnessing. Locals are often eager to share their knowledge and stories, providing valuable insights into their way of life.

Dress Appropriately: Some customs may require specific attire out of respect for tradition. Before attending any cultural events, inquire about dress codes to ensure you're dressed appropriately.

Participate With an Open Mind: Approach traditional customs with an open mind and a willingness to learn. Embrace the opportunity to step outside your comfort zone and experience something new.

Festivals and Celebrations: Throughout the year, Machu Picchu hosts a variety of festivals and celebrations, ranging from religious festivities to cultural events. These vibrant gatherings showcase music, dance, food, and art, offering visitors a glimpse into Peruvian culture.

Practical Tips for Enjoying Festivals:

Check the Calendar: Research upcoming festivals and celebrations before your trip to Machu Picchu. Planning your visit around these events allows you to experience the local culture at its most festive.

Arrive Early: Festivals can attract large crowds, so arrive early to secure a good spot and avoid missing out on any activities or performances.

Sample Local Cuisine: Festivals are an excellent opportunity to sample traditional Peruvian cuisine, including street food and regional specialties. Be adventurous and try something new!

Respect Cultural Norms: While festivals may be lively and celebratory, it's essential to respect local customs and etiquette. Pay attention to any guidelines or rules provided by event organizers.

Conclusion: Engaging with traditional customs and participating in festivals are integral parts of experiencing the cultural richness of Machu Picchu. By immersing yourself in these cultural experiences, you'll gain a deeper appreciation for the customs, traditions, and celebrations that have shaped the region for centuries. So embrace the opportunity to connect with the local community and create lasting memories during your visit to Machu Picchu!

Artisan Markets and Souvenir Shopping

Exploring artisan markets and shopping for souvenirs is an essential part of the Machu Picchu experience. These bustling markets offer a wide array of handcrafted goods, textiles, and keepsakes that reflect the rich cultural heritage of Peru.

Discovering Artisan Markets: Machu Picchu is dotted with artisan markets where local artisans showcase their craftsmanship and creativity. From colorful textiles to intricately carved ceramics, these markets are treasure troves of unique souvenirs and gifts.

Practical Tips for Navigating Artisan Markets:

Bargain Responsibly: Bargaining is common practice in Peruvian markets, but remember to do so respectfully. Start by offering a fair price and be prepared to negotiate until both parties reach a mutually agreeable deal.

Inspect Items Carefully: Take the time to examine the quality and craftsmanship of items before making a purchase. Check for any flaws or imperfections, especially in handmade goods.

Support Local Artisans: When possible, purchase directly from artisans or cooperatives to ensure your money goes directly to the creators. Look for stalls or shops that display signs indicating their products are handmade or locally sourced.

Ask About Materials and Techniques: If you're interested in learning more about a particular item, don't hesitate to ask the artisan about the materials used and the techniques involved in its creation.

Souvenir Shopping: Whether you're looking for a memento of your visit to Machu Picchu or searching for unique gifts to bring home, the markets offer an abundance of souvenir options to suit every taste and budget.

Practical Tips for Souvenir Shopping:

Consider Practicality: Choose souvenirs that are practical and easy to transport, especially if you're traveling with limited luggage space. Small items like textiles, ceramics, and jewelry make excellent souvenirs and gifts.

Think Beyond Keychains: While keychains and magnets are popular souvenirs, consider exploring other options that capture the essence of Machu Picchu. Handwoven textiles, alpaca wool products, and pottery are just a few examples of unique souvenirs available.

Plan Ahead: If you have specific souvenirs in mind, do some research beforehand to identify the best places to find them. Keep in mind that prices and selection may vary from market to market, so it's worth exploring multiple options.

Support Sustainable Practices: Look for artisans and vendors who prioritize sustainable and eco-friendly practices. Choose products made from locally sourced materials or those produced using environmentally friendly methods.

Conclusion: Exploring artisan markets and shopping for souvenirs in Machu Picchu is not only a chance to acquire unique treasures but also an opportunity to support local artisans and immerse yourself in the vibrant culture of Peru. So take your time to browse, bargain, and discover the perfect mementos to commemorate your visit to this extraordinary destination.

Music and Dance Performances

Music and dance are integral parts of Peruvian culture, and experiencing live performances in Machu Picchu can be a highlight of your visit. From traditional Andean melodies to vibrant folk dances, there are numerous opportunities to immerse yourself in the rhythms and movements of Peru.

Exploring Music and Dance Performances: Throughout Machu Picchu, you'll find venues and events showcasing traditional music and dance performances. Whether it's a small gathering in a local plaza or a larger cultural event, these performances offer a glimpse into the soul of Peruvian culture.

Practical Tips for Enjoying Music and Dance Performances:

Research Local Events: Check local event listings or ask your hotel concierge for recommendations on music and dance performances happening during your visit. Planning ahead can help you make the most of your time and ensure you don't miss out on any exciting performances.

Arrive Early: Popular performances can attract large crowds, so arrive early to secure a good spot and avoid missing the start of the show.

Respect the Performers: During performances, show respect for the performers by refraining from talking loudly or using flash photography. It's essential to remain attentive and engaged, allowing yourself to fully appreciate the cultural experience.

Participate When Invited: In some traditional dances, audience participation is encouraged. If invited to join in, embrace the opportunity to learn a few steps and immerse yourself in the joyous atmosphere.

Discovering Local Music and Dance Styles: Peru is home to a diverse array of music and dance styles, each with its own unique characteristics and cultural significance. From the haunting melodies of the Andean flute to the energetic rhythms of Afro-Peruvian drumming, there's something to captivate every audience member.

Practical Tips for Discovering Local Music and Dance Styles:

Attend Cultural Performances: Seek out performances that showcase a variety of music and dance styles, allowing you to experience the full spectrum of Peruvian culture. Look for events featuring traditional Andean music, Afro Peruvian dances, and contemporary fusion performances.

Interact with Local Musicians and Dancers: After performances, consider engaging with the performers to learn more about their art forms and cultural heritage. Many musicians and dancers are happy to share their knowledge and passion with curious audience members.

Purchase Music and Dance Souvenirs: Support local artists by purchasing CDs, DVDs, or handicrafts related to the music and dance performances you've enjoyed. These souvenirs not only serve as reminders of your cultural experiences but also contribute to the livelihoods of talented performers.

Conclusion: Attending music and dance performances in Machu Picchu offers a unique opportunity to connect with the rich cultural heritage of Peru. By immersing yourself in the rhythms, melodies, and movements of traditional Andean music and dance, you'll create unforgettable memories and gain a deeper appreciation for the cultural diversity of this remarkable region.

Chapter 7

Itineraries - One-Day Machu Picchu Experience

If you're short on time but eager to experience the wonders of Machu Picchu, a one-day itinerary can provide a fulfilling and memorable adventure. With careful planning and efficient time management, you can make the most of your visit to this iconic archaeological site.

Planning Your Itinerary: Before setting out on your one-day Machu Picchu adventure, it's essential to have a clear plan in place. Consider the following factors when crafting your itinerary:

Entry Tickets: Purchase your entry tickets to Machu Picchu in advance to avoid disappointment, as daily visitor numbers are limited. Tickets can be purchased online or in person at designated ticket offices.

Transportation: Decide how you'll reach Machu Picchu from your starting point, whether it's by train, bus, or hiking the Inca Trail. Be sure to factor in travel time and any necessary transfers.

Time of Day: Machu Picchu is typically busiest in the morning and early afternoon. Consider arriving early in the day or later in the afternoon to avoid crowds and make the most of your time.

Guided Tour: While not required, joining a guided tour can enhance your experience by providing insights into the history and significance of Machu Picchu. Choose a tour that aligns with your interests and schedule.

Practical Tips for Your One-Day Machu Picchu Experience:

Start Early: To maximize your time at Machu Picchu and enjoy the site with fewer crowds, aim to arrive early in the morning when the gates open. This also allows you to witness the sunrise over the ancient ruins, a truly magical experience.

Focus on Key Areas: With limited time available, prioritize visiting the main highlights of Machu Picchu, such as the Temple of the Sun, Intihuatana, and the Sun Gate. A guided tour can help ensure you don't miss any important sites.

Stay Hydrated and Energized: Machu Picchu's high altitude and steep terrain can be physically demanding. Bring plenty of water, snacks, and sunscreen to stay hydrated and energized throughout the day.

Take Breaks: Pace yourself and take breaks as needed to rest and soak in the breathtaking scenery. There are designated resting areas throughout the site where you can pause and admire the views.

Capture Memories: Don't forget to bring a camera or smartphone to capture photos of your Machu Picchu adventure. Be respectful of signage and regulations regarding photography, especially in sensitive areas.

Conclusion: While a one-day visit to Machu Picchu may seem short, careful planning and efficient time management can ensure you make the most of your experience. By following this itinerary and incorporating practical tips, you'll create lasting memories of your unforgettable journey to one of the world's most extraordinary archaeological sites.

Two-Day Machu Picchu Adventure

A two-day Machu Picchu adventure allows for a more leisurely exploration of this iconic archaeological site and its surrounding attractions. With an extra day at your disposal, you can delve deeper into the history, culture, and natural beauty of Machu Picchu and its environs.

Planning Your Itinerary: When crafting your two-day Machu Picchu adventure, consider the following factors to make the most of your time:

Entry Tickets: Purchase a two-day entry ticket to Machu Picchu, which allows for visits to the archaeological site on consecutive days. Ensure you have your tickets booked in advance to secure your preferred dates.

Accommodation: Arrange accommodation in Aguas Calientes, the town located at the base of Machu Picchu. Choose lodging that fits your budget and preferences, whether it's a cozy guesthouse or a luxury hotel.

Transportation: Decide how you'll reach Machu Picchu from Aguas Calientes, whether it's by bus or on foot via the Inca Trail. Factor in travel time and any additional activities you plan to undertake.

Activities and Attractions: Research other attractions in the area, such as the Machu Picchu Museum, Huayna Picchu or Machu Picchu Mountain hikes, and the thermal baths of Aguas Calientes. Determine which activities align with your interests and schedule.

Practical Tips for Your Two-Day Machu Picchu Adventure:

Day 1: Explore Machu Picchu: Begin your adventure by exploring the main archaeological site of Machu Picchu. Consider joining a guided tour to gain insights into the history and significance of the ruins. Take your time to wander through the various sectors, including the Urban Sector, Agricultural Sector, and Sacred Plaza.

Day 2: Additional Activities: On your second day, consider exploring other attractions in the area. Hike to the summit of Huayna Picchu or

Machu Picchu Mountain for panoramic views of the surrounding landscape. Visit the Machu Picchu Museum to learn more about the site's history and archaeology. Alternatively, relax and unwind in the thermal baths of Aguas Calientes after your adventures.

Pack Wisely: Ensure you have all the necessary gear and supplies for your two-day adventure, including comfortable walking shoes, sunscreen, insect repellent, and a refillable water bottle. Dress in layers to accommodate changes in temperature throughout the day.

Stay Flexible: While it's essential to have a rough itinerary in place, be open to spontaneity and unexpected discoveries along the way. Allow yourself time to linger in particularly scenic spots or engage with locals for insider tips and recommendations.

Capture Memories: Don't forget to document your two-day Machu Picchu adventure with plenty of photos and videos. Cherish the moments spent exploring this extraordinary UNESCO World Heritage Site and its surrounding wonders.

Conclusion: A two-day Machu Picchu adventure offers a more immersive and enriching experience, allowing you to explore the archaeological site at a leisurely pace and discover additional attractions in the area. By following this itinerary and incorporating practical tips, you'll create unforgettable memories of your journey to this legendary destination.

7-Day Itineraries for Exploring the Region

With a full week to explore the Machu Picchu region, you can immerse yourself in its rich history, stunning landscapes, and vibrant culture. Here are two comprehensive itineraries to help you make the most of your seven days in this extraordinary destination.

Itinerary 1: Archaeological Wonders and Cultural Experiences

Day 1: Arrival in Cusco

Arrive in Cusco, the historic capital of the Inca Empire.

Spend the day acclimatizing to the altitude and exploring the city's colonial architecture, bustling markets, and vibrant atmosphere.

Day 2: Cusco City Tour

Embark on a guided tour of Cusco's top attractions, including the Plaza de Armas, Cathedral of Santo Domingo, and Qorikancha (Temple of the Sun).

Visit nearby archaeological sites such as Sacsayhuaman, Q'enqo, Tambomachay, and Puka Pukara.

Day 3: Sacred Valley Excursion

Explore the Sacred Valley of the Incas, visiting the Pisac Archaeological Site and Market, Ollantaytambo Fortress, and Chinchero Village.

Learn about traditional Andean culture and craftsmanship through cultural demonstrations and interactions with local artisans.

Day 4: Machu Picchu Arrival

Travel to Aguas Calientes, the gateway town to Machu Picchu.

Take the afternoon to relax and prepare for your visit to the archaeological site the following day.

Day 5: Machu Picchu Exploration

Rise early to catch the first bus to Machu Picchu and witness the sunrise over the ancient ruins.

Spend the day exploring Machu Picchu's main attractions, including the Temple of the Sun, Intihuatana, and the Inca Bridge.

Consider hiking to the summit of Huayna Picchu or Machu Picchu Mountain for panoramic views of the surrounding landscape.

Day 6: Optional Activities

Choose from a variety of optional activities, such as visiting the Machu Picchu Museum, soaking in the thermal baths of Aguas Calientes, or embarking on a scenic hike in the surrounding area.

Day 7: Departure

Depart Aguas Calientes and return to Cusco to catch your onward flight or continue your travels.

Practical Tips for Exploring the Region:

Stay hydrated and pace yourself, especially when exploring high-altitude destinations like Cusco and Machu Picchu.

Dress in layers and wear comfortable walking shoes, as you'll be doing a lot of walking and may encounter varying weather conditions.

Book tickets for popular attractions and activities in advance to avoid disappointment, especially during peak tourist seasons.

Embrace the local culture and customs by interacting with locals, trying traditional Peruvian cuisine, and participating in cultural experiences and activities.

Conclusion: With a well-planned itinerary and some practical tips in mind, you can make the most of your seven days in the Machu Picchu region, exploring its archaeological wonders, cultural treasures, and natural beauty. Whether you're a history buff, adventure seeker, or culture enthusiast, there's something for everyone to enjoy in this captivating destination.

Chapter 8

Practical Tips and Advice

As you prepare for your journey to Machu Picchu, it's essential to consider some practical tips and advice to ensure a smooth and enjoyable experience. Here are some helpful suggestions to keep in mind:

Planning Your Trip:

Book in Advance: Make arrangements for accommodations, transportation, and entry tickets well in advance, especially during peak tourist seasons. This helps secure your preferred options and avoids last-minute hassles.

Check Entry Requirements: Ensure you have all necessary documents for entry into Peru and Machu Picchu, including passports, visas (if required), and entry tickets. It's also a good idea to carry copies of important documents in case of loss or theft.

Pack Wisely: Pack light but include essentials such as comfortable walking shoes, weather appropriate clothing, sunscreen, insect repellent, a refillable water bottle, and any necessary medications. Consider the high altitude and variable weather conditions when choosing clothing.

Stay Informed: Stay updated on current travel advisories, weather forecasts, and local regulations before and during your trip. Follow any safety guidelines provided by authorities and exercise caution in unfamiliar environments.

Navigating Machu Picchu:

Arrive Early: To avoid crowds and make the most of your time at Machu Picchu, aim to arrive early in the morning when the gates open. This allows for a quieter and more serene experience, especially during peak tourist hours.

Stay Hydrated: The high altitude and physical exertion of exploring Machu Picchu can lead to dehydration. Bring a refillable water bottle and drink plenty of fluids throughout the day to stay hydrated and prevent altitude sickness.

Respect the Environment: Machu Picchu is a UNESCO World Heritage Site, and it's crucial to respect its natural and cultural significance. Follow designated trails, refrain from littering, and avoid touching or damaging archaeological structures.

Take Breaks: Pace yourself and take breaks as needed to rest and recharge. There are designated resting areas throughout the site where you can pause and admire the views while catching your breath.

Engage with Guides: Consider hiring a local guide to enhance your experience and gain insights into the history, culture, and significance of Machu Picchu. Guides can provide valuable information and answer any questions you may have.

Safety and Health:

Acclimatize Properly: If traveling from sea level to high altitude destinations like Cusco and Machu Picchu, take time to acclimatize and adjust to the altitude to prevent altitude sickness. Avoid strenuous activities during the first few days and stay hydrated.

Watch Your Step: Machu Picchu's terrain can be uneven and steep, so watch your step and wear appropriate footwear with good traction to prevent slips and falls.

Protect Against Sun Exposure: The sun's rays can be strong at high altitudes, so wear sunscreen, sunglasses, and a wide-brimmed hat to protect yourself from sunburn and UV damage.

Seek Medical Assistance if Needed: If you experience symptoms of altitude sickness, dehydration, or other health concerns, seek medical assistance immediately. Machu Picchu has medical facilities available for emergencies, but it's always best to be prepared.

Conclusion: By following these practical tips and advice, you can ensure a safe, enjoyable, and memorable experience during your visit to Machu Picchu. From planning your trip to navigating the site and prioritizing your health and safety, these suggestions will help you make the most of your journey to this extraordinary destination.

Safety Precautions and Health Considerations

Health and Wellness Considerations

Ensuring your safety and well-being while visiting Machu Picchu and the surrounding region is essential for a memorable and enjoyable experience. Here are some practical safety precautions and health considerations to keep in mind during your visit:

1. **Altitude Sickness:** One of the primary health concerns for visitors to Machu Picchu is altitude sickness, also known as acute mountain sickness (AMS). Machu Picchu sits at an elevation of approximately 2,430 meters (7,970 feet) above sea level, and the surrounding peaks reach even higher altitudes. Symptoms of altitude sickness can include headache, nausea, fatigue, and shortness of breath.

Practical Tip: To minimize the risk of altitude sickness, allow yourself time to acclimatize before beginning any strenuous activities. Stay hydrated, avoid alcohol and caffeine, and consider taking medication such as acetazolamide (Diamox) if recommended by your healthcare provider.

2.   Sun Protection: The high altitude and proximity to the equator make sun protection essential when exploring Machu Picchu. The sun's rays can be intense, especially at higher elevations, increasing the risk of sunburn and heat exhaustion.

Practical Tip: Wear sunscreen with a high SPF rating, sunglasses with UV protection, and a wide-brimmed hat to shield your face and neck from the sun. Consider wearing lightweight, breathable clothing that covers your skin to reduce sun exposure.

3.   Hydration: Staying hydrated is crucial when exploring Machu Picchu, especially at higher altitudes where the air is drier and dehydration can occur more rapidly. Drink plenty of water throughout the day to replenish fluids lost through sweating and respiration.

Practical Tip: Carry a refillable water bottle and drink water regularly, even if you don't feel thirsty. Consider bringing electrolyte tablets or sports drinks to replenish lost electrolytes and prevent dehydration.

4.   Footwear and Foot Care: Proper footwear is essential for navigating the uneven terrain and steep inclines of Machu Picchu and its surrounding trails. Ill-fitting or inadequate footwear can lead to blisters, foot pain, and injuries.

Practical Tip: Wear sturdy, comfortable hiking boots or trail shoes with good traction and ankle support. Break in your footwear before your trip to avoid discomfort and blisters. Pack blister prevention products such as moleskin or blister pads in case of emergency.

5.   First Aid Kit: Carrying a basic first aid kit with essential supplies can be invaluable in case of minor injuries or medical emergencies while exploring Machu Picchu and its surroundings.

Practical Tip: Pack a first aid kit containing adhesive bandages, gauze pads, antiseptic wipes, adhesive tape, pain relievers, anti-inflammatory medication, blister treatment, insect repellent, and any personal medications you may need.

Familiarize yourself with the contents of your first aid kit and how to use them effectively.

By following these safety precautions and health considerations, you can enjoy a safe and fulfilling experience while exploring Machu Picchu and the stunning landscapes of the Andes. Prioritize your well-being and take proactive measures to mitigate potential risks, allowing you to fully immerse yourself in the wonders of this iconic destination.

Responsible Tourism Practices

Responsible tourism is essential for preserving the natural beauty, cultural heritage, and ecological integrity of Machu Picchu and its surrounding areas. As visitors, it's crucial to adopt sustainable and ethical practices to minimize our impact on the environment and support local communities. Here are some practical tips for responsible tourism:

1. **Respect Local Culture and Customs:** Show respect for the customs, traditions, and beliefs of the local communities you encounter during your visit to Machu Picchu. Ask for permission before taking photographs of people or sacred sites, and dress modestly when visiting religious or cultural landmarks.

Practical Tip: Take the time to learn about the history and cultural significance of Machu Picchu and its surrounding areas, and engage with local guides and community members to gain a deeper understanding of their way of life.

2. **Minimize Waste and Reduce Plastic Use:** Reduce your environmental footprint by minimizing waste and avoiding single-use plastics during your visit. Bring a reusable water bottle, refill it from water stations or purified sources, and avoid purchasing drinks or snacks packaged in plastic.

Practical Tip: Pack a reusable shopping bag and utensils to minimize waste when purchasing souvenirs or enjoying meals on the go. Dispose of litter responsibly and participate in organized clean-up efforts to help keep Machu Picchu and its surrounding areas pristine.

3.   Support Local Businesses and Artisans: Support the local economy by patronizing locally owned businesses, restaurants, and artisan markets. Purchase souvenirs and handicrafts directly from local artisans, ensuring that your money directly benefits the communities you visit.

Practical Tip: Seek out community-based tourism initiatives and sustainable tourism operators that prioritize environmental conservation and support local development projects. By choosing responsible tour operators, you can contribute to positive social and economic impacts in the region.

4.   Stay on Designated Trails and Respect Wildlife: Protect fragile ecosystems and wildlife habitats by staying on designated trails and avoiding trampling vegetation or disturbing wildlife. Observe animals from a safe distance and refrain from feeding or approaching them to minimize stress and disruption to their natural behavior.

Practical Tip: Follow the principles of Leave No Trace ethics, including packing out all trash, avoiding picking plants or flowers, and refraining from leaving behind any markings or graffiti. By treading lightly and leaving natural areas undisturbed, you can help preserve the integrity of Machu Picchu for future generations.

5.   Conserve Water and Energy:
Conserve water and energy resources during your stay by taking shorter showers, turning off lights and electronics when not in use, and opting for ecofriendly accommodation options that prioritize sustainable practices.

Practical Tip: Conserve water by reusing towels and linens during your stay and taking shorter showers to minimize water usage. Choose accommodations that have implemented energy-saving measures such as solar panels or energy-efficient appliances.

By embracing responsible tourism practices, you can contribute to the long-term sustainability and preservation of Machu Picchu and its surrounding areas. By adopting environmentally friendly behaviors and supporting local communities, you can help ensure that future generations can continue to enjoy this iconic destination for years to come.

Chapter 9

Beyond Machu Picchu - Nearby Attractions and Day Trips

While Machu Picchu is undoubtedly the highlight of any visit to the region, there are plenty of other attractions and day trip options to explore in the surrounding area. Here are some recommendations for extending your adventure beyond Machu Picchu:

1. Sacred Valley of the Incas: The Sacred Valley, or Valle Sagrado, is a picturesque region nestled between Cusco and Machu Picchu, known for its stunning landscapes, charming villages, and ancient Inca ruins. Visit the agricultural terraces of Moray, the salt mines of Maras, and the fortress of Ollantaytambo to immerse yourself in the rich history and culture of the Inca civilization.

Practical Tip: Consider hiring a local guide or joining a guided tour to explore the Sacred Valley, as they can provide valuable insights into the region's history and culture. Bring plenty of water, sunscreen, and comfortable walking shoes for exploring archaeological sites and hiking trails.

2. **Maras Salt Mines:** The Maras Salt Mines, or Salineras de Maras, are a series of terraced salt pans dating back to Inca times, where salt

has been harvested for centuries using traditional methods. Explore the labyrinth of salt pools and learn about the ancient techniques used to extract salt from the mineral-rich spring waters.

Practical Tip: Wear sturdy footwear with good traction, as the paths around the salt mines can be uneven and slippery. Bring a camera to capture the striking contrast of the white salt pans against the surrounding Andean landscape.

3. **Moray Agricultural Terraces:** The circular agricultural terraces of Moray are an engineering marvel built by the Incas for experimental farming and crop cultivation. Explore the concentric rings of terraces and marvel at the ingenuity of ancient agricultural practices that allowed the Incas to grow a variety of crops at different altitudes.

Practical Tip: Bring a hat and sunscreen to protect yourself from the sun while exploring the exposed terraces of Moray. Take your time to wander through the terraces and appreciate the panoramic views of the surrounding mountains and valleys.

4. **Pisac Archaeological Site and Market:**
   The town of Pisac is home to an impressive
   Inca archaeological site perched on a hilltop
   overlooking the Sacred Valley. Explore the
   ruins of temples, terraces, and residential
   areas, then visit the bustling Pisac Market to
   shop for handmade crafts, textiles, and
   souvenirs.

Practical Tip: Arrive early to beat the crowds
and explore the Pisac archaeological site before
it gets too hot. Bargain with local vendors at the
market to get the best deals on handmade goods
and support the local economy.

5. **Aguas Calientes Hot Springs:** After a day
   of exploring archaeological sites and hiking
   trails, unwind and relax at the Aguas Calientes
   hot springs. Located just a short distance from
   Machu Picchu Pueblo, these natural thermal

baths offer soothing waters and stunning views of the surrounding mountains.

Practical Tip: Bring a swimsuit, towel, and change of clothes for your visit to the hot springs. Consider visiting in the evening to enjoy the tranquil atmosphere and soak in the warm waters under the starry sky.

Exploring the attractions and day trip options beyond Machu Picchu allows you to experience the diverse landscapes, rich history, and vibrant culture of the Sacred Valley and its surrounding areas. Whether you're interested in ancient ruins, traditional markets, or natural hot springs, there's something for everyone to enjoy in this enchanting region of Peru.

Additional Destinations in Peru

While Machu Picchu is undoubtedly one of

Peru's most iconic attractions, the country offers a wealth of other destinations waiting to be explored. From vibrant cities to remote wilderness areas, here are some additional destinations in Peru to consider adding to your itinerary:

1. **Cusco:** As the former capital of the Inca Empire, Cusco is a fascinating blend of ancient history and colonial architecture. Explore the cobblestone streets of the historic center, visit the impressive Cathedral and Coricancha Temple, and browse the vibrant markets selling handicrafts and textiles.

Practical Tip: Spend at least a few days exploring Cusco and acclimating to the altitude before embarking on any treks or hikes to Machu Picchu. Take it slow, stay hydrated, and consider drinking coca tea to alleviate symptoms of altitude sickness.

2. Arequipa: Known as the "White City" for its colonial-era buildings made of white volcanic stone, Arequipa is a charming city located in the southern part of Peru. Explore the historic center, visit the Santa Catalina Monastery, and venture into the nearby Colca Canyon to spot Andean condors soaring overhead.

Practical Tip: Take a guided tour of the Santa Catalina Monastery to learn about its fascinating history and architectural features. If you're feeling adventurous, consider hiking or biking in the surrounding countryside to enjoy stunning views of the Andes.

3. Lake Titicaca: Straddling the border between Peru and Bolivia, Lake Titicaca is the highest navigable lake in the world and home to indigenous communities that have lived on its shores for centuries. Take a boat tour to the Uros Islands, where locals live on floating reed islands, and visit Taquile Island to learn about traditional Andean culture and textiles.

Practical Tip: Spend a night on one of the floating reed islands to experience traditional Andean hospitality and learn about the unique way of life of the Uros people. Don't forget to bring warm clothing, as temperatures can be chilly, especially at night.

4. **Amazon Rainforest:** For an unforgettable wilderness adventure, consider visiting the Peruvian Amazon Rainforest. Take a guided jungle tour to spot exotic wildlife such as monkeys, sloths, and colorful birds, and learn about the diverse plant life and ecosystems of the Amazon.

Practical Tip: Choose a reputable tour operator that follows sustainable and ecofriendly practices to minimize impact on the fragile Amazon ecosystem. Pack lightweight, breathable clothing, insect repellent, and sunscreen for your jungle excursions.

5. **Nazca Lines:** Marvel at the mysterious

Nazca Lines, a series of ancient geoglyphs etched into the desert floor of southern Peru. Take a scenic flight over the Nazca Desert to see the intricate designs, including geometric shapes, animals, and humanoid figures, that have puzzled archaeologists for centuries.

Practical Tip: Book a flight with a reputable airline that prioritizes safety and provides informative commentary during the flight to help you understand the significance of the Nazca Lines. Bring a camera with a zoom lens to capture clear images of the geoglyphs from the air.

Exploring these additional destinations in Peru allows you to experience the country's diverse landscapes, rich cultural heritage, and unique attractions beyond Machu Picchu. Whether you're interested in history, nature, or adventure, Peru has something to offer every traveler seeking an unforgettable experience.

Extending Your Trip: Tips for Further Exploration

While Machu Picchu is undoubtedly the crown jewel of Peru, extending your trip to explore more of this diverse and captivating country is highly recommended. Here are some practical tips for further exploration:

1. **Research and Plan Ahead:** Before extending your trip, take the time to research other destinations in Peru that align with your

interests and travel preferences. Consider factors such as weather, transportation options, and accommodation availability when planning your itinerary.

Practical Tip: Use reputable travel websites, guidebooks, and online forums to gather information and recommendations from fellow travelers who have explored other regions of Peru. Create a detailed itinerary with a mix of must-see attractions and off-the-beaten-path experiences.

2. Consider Your Interests and Preferences: Think about what activities and experiences you enjoy most when planning your extended trip. Whether you're interested in history, culture, nature, or adventure, Peru offers a wide range of options to suit every traveler's interests.

Practical Tip: Make a list of activities and attractions that you're most excited about, and prioritize them based on your preferences and available time. Be open to trying new things and exploring areas that may not be as well-known but offer unique experiences.

3. **Allow for Flexibility in Your Itinerary:** While it's essential to have a well-planned itinerary, allow for some flexibility to adapt to unexpected circumstances or opportunities that may arise during your trip. Embrace spontaneity and be open to changing your plans based on local recommendations or last-minute discoveries.

Practical Tip: Build in buffer days in your itinerary to account for delays, weather disruptions, or impromptu detours. Leave room for relaxation and downtime to avoid feeling rushed or overwhelmed by a packed schedule.

4. **Stay Safe and Informed:** As you extend your trip to explore other regions of Peru,

prioritize your safety and well-being at all times.

Stay informed about local customs, safety advisories, and travel restrictions, and take precautions to protect yourself and your belongings.

Practical Tip: Stay connected with reliable sources of information such as travel advisories from your home country's embassy or consulate, local news outlets, and official tourism websites. Be aware of your surroundings, trust your instincts, and avoid risky or unsafe situations.

5. Embrace Local Experiences and Connections: One of the most rewarding aspects of travel is connecting with local people and immersing yourself in the culture and traditions of the places you visit. Take the time to interact with locals, sample regional cuisine, and participate in cultural activities to gain a deeper appreciation for Peru's rich heritage.

Practical Tip: Seek out opportunities to engage with local communities through homestays, cooking classes, volunteer programs, or guided tours led by knowledgeable local guides. Be respectful, curious, and open-minded as you learn from the people you meet along the way.

By following these practical tips for further exploration, you can extend your trip beyond Machu Picchu and uncover the many treasures that Peru has to offer. Whether you're exploring ancient ruins, hiking through pristine wilderness, or sampling delicious cuisine, embrace the adventure and make the most of your time in this remarkable country.

Chapter 10

Resources - Useful Websites and Online Resources

In today's digital age, the internet provides a wealth of information and resources to help you plan and enhance your travel experience to Machu Picchu and Peru. Here are some useful websites and online resources to assist you:

1. Official Tourism Websites:

Peru. Travel: The official website of the Peru Tourism Board offers comprehensive information on travel destinations, attractions, activities, and practical travel tips for visiting Peru.

VisitPeru.com: Another official tourism website of Peru provides valuable insights into Peru's diverse regions, cultural heritage, and travel itineraries.

Practical Tip: Explore these websites to familiarize yourself with Peru's top attractions, recommended itineraries, and travel advisories before planning your trip.

2. Travel Forums and Online Communities:

TripAdvisor Forums: Join discussions on the Machu Picchu and Peru forums to seek advice, share experiences, and connect with fellow travelers for tips and recommendations.

Lonely Planet Thorn Tree Forum: Engage with other travelers on the Thorn Tree forum to exchange information, ask questions, and gather insights into traveling in Peru.

Practical Tip: Participate in online forums to get firsthand advice from experienced travelers, learn about hidden gems, and troubleshoot any travel-related concerns or questions.

3. Booking Platforms and Aggregators:
Booking.com, Airbnb, and Expedia: Use these platforms to search and book accommodations,

tours, and activities in Machu Picchu and Peru, with options ranging from budget-friendly hostels to luxury hotels.

Skyscanner and Kayak: Compare flight prices, routes, and schedules to find the best deals on airfare for your journey to Peru.

Practical Tip: Take advantage of user reviews, ratings, and photos on booking platforms to make informed decisions and ensure a comfortable and enjoyable travel experience.

4. Government and Official Websites:

U.S. Department of State - Travel Advisories: Check for travel advisories, safety alerts, and entry requirements for Peru on the official website of the U.S. Department of State or your country's equivalent government website. Peru Ministry of Culture: Visit the official website of the Peru Ministry of Culture for information on archaeological sites, entrance fees, and regulations for visiting Machu Picchu and other cultural attractions.

Practical Tip: Stay updated on travel advisories and safety guidelines issued by official government sources to ensure a smooth and hassle-free trip to Machu Picchu and Peru.

5. Travel Blogs and Online Guides:

The Culture Trip, Nomadic Matt, and The Points Guy: Explore travel blogs and online guides for firsthand travel experiences, destination insights, and practical tips from seasoned travelers and experts.

National Geographic Travel: Discover in-depth articles, photography, and travel guides on Machu Picchu and Peru from National Geographic Travel's website.

Practical Tip: Read travel blogs and online guides to gain inspiration, learn insider tips, and uncover hidden gems for your trip to Machu Picchu and Peru.

By leveraging these useful websites and online resources, you can enhance your travel planning process, access valuable information, and make the most of your journey to Machu Picchu and the enchanting landscapes of Peru.

Emergency Contacts

When traveling to Machu Picchu and Peru, it's essential to be prepared for any unforeseen circumstances or emergencies that may arise during your trip. Here are some important emergency contacts to keep handy:

1. Emergency Services:

Police: Dial 105 to reach the police in Peru for emergencies, such as theft, accidents, or incidents requiring immediate assistance.

Ambulance: Dial 117 to request an ambulance in case of medical emergencies or accidents requiring urgent medical attention.

Fire Department: Dial 116 to reach the fire department for emergencies such as fires, rescues, or hazardous situations.

Practical Tip: Save these emergency numbers in your phone contacts and familiarize yourself with basic Spanish phrases to communicate effectively in case of an emergency.

2. Medical Assistance:

Tourist Police: In tourist areas like Machu Picchu and Cusco, there are specialized tourist police units who can provide assistance and guidance to travelers in distress.

Local Hospitals and Clinics: Research and note down the contact information for nearby hospitals, clinics, and medical facilities in the areas you plan to visit.

Practical Tip: Purchase travel insurance that includes coverage for medical emergencies, evacuation, and repatriation to ensure you receive timely and adequate medical care if needed.

3. Consulate or Embassy:

U.S. Embassy in Lima: In case of emergencies involving U.S. citizens, contact the U.S. Embassy in Lima for assistance, including replacement of lost or stolen passports, legal aid, and emergency financial assistance.

Embassy or Consulate of your home country: If you're not a U.S. citizen, locate and note down the contact information for the embassy or consulate of your home country in Peru.

Practical Tip: Register with your embassy or consulate through their online registration system to receive important updates, travel advisories, and assistance during your stay in Peru.

4. Tour Operator or Accommodation:

Contact your tour operator or accommodation provider for assistance in case of emergencies, such as natural disasters, transportation disruptions, or security concerns.

Keep a copy of your itinerary and contact details for your tour operator or accommodation provider readily accessible.

Practical Tip: Inform your tour operator or accommodation provider of any medical conditions, allergies, or special requirements before your trip to ensure they can assist you appropriately in case of an emergency.

5. Local Contacts:

Save the contact information for local guides, tour operators, or friends you may have in Peru who can provide assistance or guidance in case of emergencies.

Consider downloading offline maps or GPS apps to navigate and locate nearby resources or facilities in areas with limited internet or phone connectivity.

Practical Tip: Establish a communication plan with your travel companions and designate a meeting point in case you get separated during emergencies or evacuation situations.

By keeping these essential emergency contacts handy and taking proactive measures to prepare for unforeseen situations, you can travel with confidence and peace of mind, knowing that you're equipped to handle emergencies effectively while exploring Machu Picchu and Peru.

Glossary of Common Terms

When planning a trip to Machu Picchu and exploring Peru, you may encounter various terms and phrases that are unique to the region or specific to travel and tourism. Here's a glossary of common terms to help you navigate your journey with ease:

1. **Machu Picchu:** A 15th-century Inca citadel located in the Andes Mountains of Peru, known for its stunning architecture, archaeological significance, and breathtaking mountain scenery.

2. **Inca Trail:** A famous hiking trail that leads to Machu Picchu, following ancient Inca pathways through the Andes Mountains and passing through diverse landscapes and archaeological sites.

3. **Altitude Sickness:** Also known as acute mountain sickness (AMS), it is a condition caused by reduced air pressure and lower oxygen levels at high altitudes, resulting in

symptoms such as headache, nausea, dizziness, and fatigue.

4. **Llama:** A domesticated South American camelid commonly found in the Andes Mountains of Peru, known for its woolly coat, long neck, and distinctive appearance.

5. **Pisco Sour:** Peru's national cocktail made with pisco (a grape brandy), lime juice, simple syrup, egg white, and bitters, often served as a refreshing drink in bars and restaurants throughout the country.

6. **Quechua:** The indigenous language spoken by the Quechua people of the Andes region, including Peru, Ecuador, Bolivia, and parts of Colombia and Argentina.

7. **Plaza de Armas:** The main square or central plaza in many Peruvian cities and

towns, typically surrounded by colonial-era buildings, churches, and government offices.

8. Inti Raymi: An ancient Inca festival celebrated in Cusco and other Andean communities to honor the sun god Inti, featuring colorful processions, traditional music and dance, and ceremonial rituals.

9. Alpaca: Another domesticated South American camelid similar to the llama but smaller in size, prized for its soft and luxurious wool used in textiles and clothing.

10. Ceviche: A popular Peruvian dish made with fresh raw fish or seafood marinated in citrus juices (typically lime or lemon) and mixed with onions, chili peppers, and cilantro, served as a refreshing appetizer or main course.

Practical Tip: Familiarize yourself with these common terms and phrases to enhance your understanding and appreciation of Peruvian culture, cuisine, and traditions during your visit to Machu Picchu and beyond.

By incorporating these common terms into your vocabulary, you'll be better equipped to communicate, navigate, and immerse yourself in the rich tapestry of experiences that Peru has to offer.

Conclusion - Farewell to Machu Picchu

As your journey to Machu Picchu and Peru draws to a close, it's time to reflect on the unforgettable experiences you've had and bid farewell to this magnificent destination. Here are some final thoughts and recommendations to take with you as you depart:

Reflect on Your Journey: Take a moment to reflect on the awe-inspiring beauty of Machu Picchu, the rich cultural heritage of Peru, and the memories you've created during your travels.

Cherish the moments of wonder and discovery that have enriched your life and expanded your horizons.

Practical Tip: Keep a travel journal or create a photo album to preserve your memories and capture the essence of your journey to Machu Picchu and Peru. Write down your thoughts, feelings, and impressions to revisit and share with others in the future.

Embrace the Spirit of Adventure: Whether you explored ancient ruins, hiked through breathtaking landscapes, or sampled delicious cuisine, embrace the spirit of adventure that has fueled your travels in Peru. Celebrate your achievements and the personal growth you've experienced along the way.

Practical Tip: Stay open to new experiences and continue seeking out opportunities for exploration and discovery in your future travels. Maintain a sense of curiosity and wonder as you embark on new adventures around the world.

Express Gratitude: Take a moment to express gratitude for the people you've met, the friendships you've formed, and the hospitality you've received during your time in Peru. Thank the local guides, artisans, and communities who have shared their culture, traditions, and stories with you.

Practical Tip: Leave positive reviews and recommendations for the accommodations, tour operators, and businesses you've enjoyed during your travels. Support local artisans by purchasing handmade crafts and souvenirs to commemorate your trip.

Plan Your Next Adventure: While saying goodbye to Machu Picchu and Peru may be bittersweet, let it inspire you to start dreaming and planning your next adventure. Whether it's exploring another corner of the world or returning to Peru to uncover more hidden treasures, the possibilities are endless.

Practical Tip: Set aside time to research and plan your next travel destination, taking into account your interests, budget, and travel goals. Consider joining travel forums or groups to connect with like-minded adventurers and exchange tips and recommendations.

As you bid farewell to Machu Picchu and Peru, carry with you the memories, lessons, and experiences that have enriched your journey. May your travels continue to inspire and uplift you, wherever your adventures may take you next. Until we meet again, farewell, and safe travels!

Made in the USA
Las Vegas, NV
18 September 2024

95478394R00079